MONEY

The History of Money

Julie Haydon

Smart Apple Media

This edition first published in 2006 in the United States of America by Smart Apple Media.

All rights reserved. No part of this book may be reproduced in any form or by any means without written permission from the Publisher.

Smart Apple Media
2140 Howard Drive West
North Mankato
Minnesota 56003

First published in 2006 by
MACMILLAN EDUCATION AUSTRALIA PTY LTD
627 Chapel Street, South Yarra, Australia 3141

Visit our Web site at www.macmillan.com.au

Associated companies and representatives throughout the world.

Copyright © Julie Haydon 2006

Library of Congress Cataloging-in-Publication Data

Haydon, Julie.
  The history of money / Julie Haydon.
  p. cm. — (Money)
  Includes index.
  ISBN-13: 978-1-58340-780-6
  1. Money—History--Juvenile literature. I. Title. II. Money (Smart Apple Media)

  HG221.5.H39 2006
  332.4'9—dc22   2005057575

Edited by Miriana Dasovic
Text and cover design by Raul Diche
Page layout by Raul Diche
Photo research by Legend Images
Illustrations by Ann Likhovetsky

Printed in USA

Acknowledgments

The author and the publisher are grateful to the following for permission to reproduce copyright material:

Cover photograph: Ancient electrum coins, courtesy of Australian Picture Library/Corbis; background image courtesy of Photodisc.

American Express, p. 29; Australian Picture Library/Corbis, pp. 8, 11, 12, 14, 16; Bureau of Engraving and Printing, United States Department of the Treasury, pp. 17, 25 (both); Commonwealth Bank of Australia, p. 28; Comstock, © 2005 JupiterImages Corporation, pp. 15, 20; Coo-ee Picture Library, p. 22; AAMIR QURESHI/AFP/Getty Images, p. 18; National Australia Bank, p. 5; Photodisc, pp. 3, 32; Photolibrary, p. 23; Photolibrary/Index Stock Imagery, p. 4; Photoobjects, © 2005 JupiterImages Corporation, pp. 13, 21, 26, 27; Reserve Bank of Australia, pp. 19, 24 (both).

While every care has been taken to trace and acknowledge copyright, the publisher tenders their apologies for any accidental infringement where copyright has proved untraceable. Where the attempt has been unsuccessful, the publisher welcomes information that would redress the situation.

Contents

Glossary words

When a word is printed in **bold**, you can look up its meaning in the glossary on page 31.

What is money?

Money is what we use to pay for things. We use money to buy **products**, such as food, clothes and toys. We use money to pay for **services**, such as a train ride or a visit to the doctor. We also use money to pay **debts**.

Coins and bills

Coins and bills are forms of money. Governments make coins and bills from small amounts of paper, plastic, or metal. These materials are not worth much on their own, so a government gives each coin and bill a **value**. That way everyone knows what their coins and bills are worth, and can use them to make and accept payments. Coins and bills are also called cash.

Info-plus!

Most people use money every day. Coins and bills are convenient forms of money because they are easy to carry, use and recognise.

People often use cash to pay for small purchases, such as takeout food.

Other forms of money

Coins and bills are not the only forms of money. Sometimes people make payments with checks, credit cards or money they have in the bank.

Checks are pieces of paper that have written instructions and a signature on them. The instructions tell a bank who to pay and how much to pay. The bank takes the amount from the bank account of the **drawer**.

Credit cards are pieces of plastic that have numbers, names, a signature, and a magnetic stripe on them. People can use credit cards to buy something now and pay for it later.

Many people keep money in bank accounts. Computers at banks keep a record of how much money is in each account. The computers record every deposit, when money goes into an account, and every withdrawal, when money goes out of an account.

Info-plus!

Using computers, people can deposit or withdraw money from their bank accounts electronically.

Credit cards are made of light plastic, and fit easily into a wallet or pocket.

Bartering

Long ago, money as we know it today did not exist. Early humans moved from place to place, following the animals they hunted. There were no shops or banks. Instead, people would exchange products and services for other products and services. This is known as bartering.

Imagine that a hunter had some animal skins but wanted some fish. The hunter had to find a person who had fish and who wanted animal skins. They would then barter some skins for some fish. No money was involved. Instead, the people worked out what they thought was a fair exchange of their products.

Village life

Later, humans began growing their own food and raising farm animals. Groups of people built homes near each other, and villages began. Farmers were able to grow enough food to feed the villagers. People who did not have to grow their own food had time to develop different skills, such as weaving and pottery. They bartered their products and services with each other and with people from other villages.

Long ago, people used to barter products such as animal skins and fish.

Problems with bartering

There were problems with bartering. Imagine that a farmer had two chickens and wanted to buy a large rug, but the weaver wanted three chickens for the rug. If the **traders** could not agree on the value of their goods, no exchange could take place.

Perhaps the weaver wanted a basket of fruit instead of chickens. The farmer would first have to find a fruit grower to barter the chickens for fruit, and then return to the weaver to barter the fruit for the rug. Finding a person who had what you wanted, and wanted what you had, was sometimes difficult and time consuming.

Another problem with bartering was what to do with products that no one wanted. Coins and bills can be stored, but products such as food do not last. Other products, such as furniture, take up a lot of storage space. Services cannot be stored at all.

2 chickens ≠ rug

Bartering only worked if both traders agreed on the value of their goods.

Using products as money

Over time, people began to prefer certain products for bartering. Products that became popular included farm animals, grain, rice, salt, cloth, simple tools, and shells. People agreed on the value of these products, and these products became the first types of money.

Some products were popular as money because they were useful. Farm animals gave people meat, milk, eggs, skins, wool, and feathers. They could also be used to do labour and to breed more animals. Grain, rice, and other foods could be eaten. Cloth could be made into clothes and soft furnishings. Tools made many jobs easier.

Some products were popular partly because they looked good. Small colorful shells, called cowrie shells, were pretty and could be made into ornaments.

Info-plus!

For thousands of years, cattle were used as money. In many places, a person's wealth depended on how many cattle they owned. Even today, some people keep cattle as a sign of wealth and use them as money.

Cowrie shells were popular as money because they could be made into ornaments, such as this head-dress.

Problems with using products as money

As people travelled further to barter their products and services, they had problems with using products as money. Imagine that a farmer with a horse to barter wanted products from several traders. How could the farmer divide the horse between the traders? Or imagine that a trader came from a country where cowrie shells were common and not highly valued, and would not accept the shells in exchange for products.

Many products used as money had some disadvantages:

- They were hard to transport
- They were hard to count
- They were difficult to divide
- They spoiled or damaged easily
- They needed to be cared for
- They were not accepted everywhere

People needed a form of money that would be easy to use, keep, and transport. The new money also had to be accepted by everyone.

Info-plus!

In some tribes, special kinds of money were not used for everyday goods. Instead, they were used as gifts, to pay fines, or in important ceremonies, such as weddings.

A farmer using a horse as money could not divide the horse between several traders.

The first metal money

Metals such as copper, bronze, silver, gold, **electrum**, and iron were discovered long ago. People learned to make tools, weapons, decorations, and other items from metals. Metals were valued because they were rare, useful, long lasting, and attractive. When people realized that metals would make a good form of payment, metal money was invented.

Metal money was much better than bartered goods. It was easy to transport, weigh, divide, count, and store. It did not spoil or damage easily, and was accepted almost everywhere.

The value of a piece of metal depended upon its weight, not its size or shape. Metal was weighed on an instrument called a balance. The metal was placed on a pan on one side of the balance. Weights were added to the pan on the other side until the two pans were level. By counting the weights, it was possible to work out how heavy the piece of metal was.

Ancient metal weights were often made in the shape of animals, such as bulls and lions.

Precious metals

Gold and silver are **precious metals**. They have been used to make jewelry and other expensive products for thousands of years. Gold is usually more valuable than silver. This is because gold is thought to be more beautiful, is usually harder to find, and does not lose its shine like silver.

People began making money out of gold and silver long before coins were invented. Like other metals, the gold or silver was melted and made into small pieces, usually into bars, called ingots. When the gold or silver was handed over as money, it was weighed so its value could be decided.

In ancient cultures, it was probably only the rich and powerful who used gold and silver as money. Poor people could not afford the precious metals. They would have used products as money, or cheaper metals, such as copper and bronze.

Gold has been used to make jewelry, such as this queen's collar, for thousands of years.

Info-plus!

Many ancient cultures admired gold because its color resembled the sun.

The introduction of coins

The first coins were invented during the 600s B.C. in Turkey, which was then known as Lydia. The Lydians realized it was easier to count metal pieces of a set value than to weigh each piece. They made metal pieces of fixed weights, and stamped them with designs to show their value as money. From Lydia, the idea of coins spread to other places.

The Lydians made their coins from electrum, which is a natural mixture of gold and silver. They found the electrum in their local river. The Lydian coins did not look much like modern coins. They were rough lumps of yellow metal, with simple designs stamped on their sides. Stamping a blank piece of metal with designs is called minting.

These ancient electrum coins from Lydia look very different from modern coins.

Info-plus!

When the Lydians were inventing electrum coins, the Chinese began making bronze coins that looked like small knives and spades.

Coins of silver and gold

One problem with electrum coins was that people did not know how much gold was in each coin. Gold was more valuable than silver. The Lydians solved this problem by minting coins of pure gold and pure silver. Soon, other places were minting their own gold and silver coins, but gold coins were still much rarer than silver coins.

Modern coins

Over time, coins changed into the types of coins used today. Modern coins are made from cheap metals at **mints**. The value of a modern coin does not come from the value of its material. Instead, it comes from the value it is given by the government that **issues** it. People accept this value and use coins as money.

These Canadian 25-cent coins all look identical because they were made by machines.

Info-plus!

The side of a coin that bears the main design is called the obverse. The other side is called the reverse.

13

Bills

Coins are useful for small purchases and as small change, but carrying large amounts of coins is not convenient. Bills are light to carry and easy to fold. Like coins, their value does not depend upon their weight. This means they can be issued in different **denominations**, and in common materials, such as paper or plastic.

Paper money was first used in China over a thousand years ago. However, it was many hundreds of years before paper money was used elsewhere. By the 1700s, printed bills were being issued by banks in various countries. The bills were **receipts** for gold and silver. The receipts could be used to pay for products and services, and to repay debts. A person could take a bill to the bank and have it changed back into precious metal at any time.

This $5 note from the United States was issued in 1864.

In many places around the world, money has developed in the following way.

Barter → Products as money → Weighed metal as money → Coins

14

Modern bills

Today, governments control the making and issuing of bills. Modern bills contain the name of the issuer, the denomination of the note, images, patterns, and security features that make the note hard to copy. The images on bills often show people, animals or buildings from the issuing country.

Some bills are printed on paper, as in the United States and Canada. Others are printed on plastic, or polymer, as in Australia and New Zealand.

Modern bills are legal money, known as legal tender, because the issuing government says they are. The value of modern bills and coins is based on trust, and backed by law. Everyone, including the government, is supposed to accept them as money.

Info-plus!

The United States dollar, or "greenback," is popular in many countries outside the United States. It is used even in countries where it is not legal tender, because people are happy to accept it and trust its value.

Unlike early bills, modern bills are not receipts for other items.

Paper money → Modern bills and checks → Plastic cards and electronic money

Making coins and bills

There are many stages in making coins and bills. The process requires planning, and needs a variety of materials, sophisticated machines, and skilled workers.

How coins are minted

To make coins, the designs are first drawn, and the **dies** are made and put into the **coining press**. Then the **blanks** are made. Finally, the coins are minted, as shown in the flowchart below.

Designing the dies

The theme for the coin is chosen.

↓

The designs for the coin are drawn.

↓

Large models of the coin are made.

↓

The dies are made.

↓

The dies are put into the coining press.

Making the blanks

The blanking press cuts blanks from strips of metal.

↓

The blanks are heated, cooled, washed, polished, and dried.

↓

The blanks go into the upsetting machine.

↓

The upsetting machine raises a rim around the edges of the blanks.

↓

The blanks go into the coining press.

At the coining press

In the coining press, both sides of the blanks are hit by dies at the same time. This makes coins.

↓

The new coins are checked and counted.

↓

The coins are put into bags that are weighed.

↓

The bags of coins are safely stored until they are transported to banks.

These blanks will be used to make 50-centime euro coins.

How bills are printed

Bills are printed on huge printing machines at a bill printer. The process is shown below.

```
The theme for the bill is chosen.
        ↓
The designs for the bill are drawn.
        ↓
The dies are made.
        ↓
The dies are used to make the
printing plates.
        ↓
The printing plates and inks are put into
several different printing machines.
        ↓
The design is printed on sheets of paper
or polymer by different printing machines.
        ↓
The sheets of new bills are cut into
individual bills.
        ↓
The bills are put into containers and
counted.
        ↓
Damaged or poorly printed bills are
removed.
        ↓
The bills are wrapped.
        ↓
The wrapped bills are safely stored until
they are transported to banks.
```

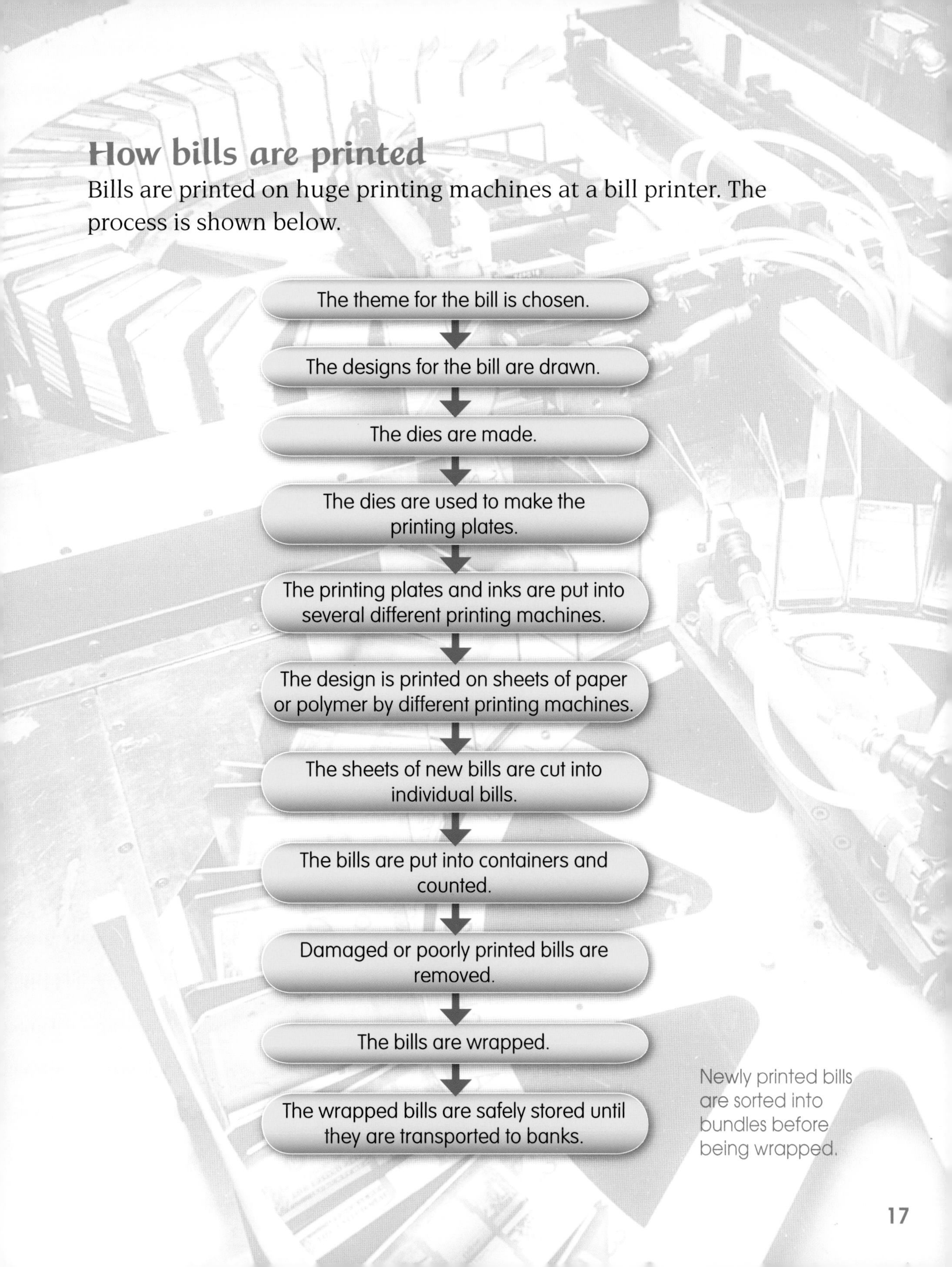

Newly printed bills are sorted into bundles before being wrapped.

Governments and money

Only governments are allowed to make and issue coins and bills. Governments decide how many coins and bills to make.

Currencies

Most countries have their own type of money. A type of money is called a currency. The value of a currency depends on how much of another currency can be bought with it.

Governments work hard to keep their currencies safe. One way to do this is to control the making and issuing of coins and bills. If a country's currency is trusted, it will have a high value in the world, and people will use it. If everyone started making coins and bills, then a currency would lose its value. Prices would go up. People would no longer have to work to earn money, so jobs would not be done. Nobody would want money for products and services, or as payment for debts. People's savings would be worthless.

These fake United States bills were found during a police raid in Pakistan.

Security features

Coins and bills are designed with security features that are easy to check but difficult to counterfeit, or copy illegally, without the proper materials and equipment. Mints and bill printers guard their materials and equipment closely.

United States' $20 bill

There are many security features on the $20 bill.

The bill is printed on special paper that contains red and blue fibers, so the paper looks different from other types of paper.

A watermark, or faint image, is part of the paper. It can be seen from both sides of the bill.

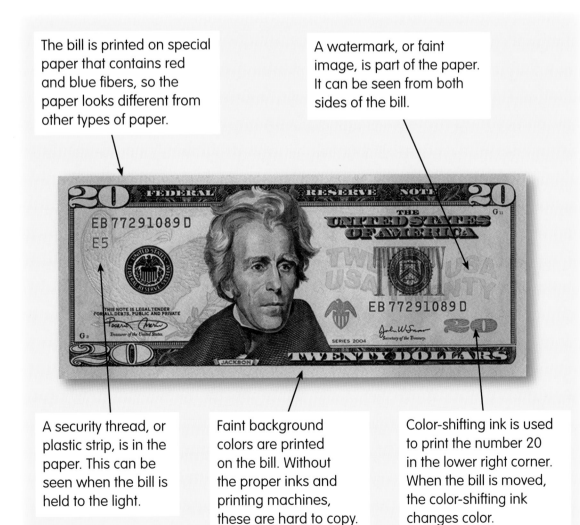

A security thread, or plastic strip, is in the paper. This can be seen when the bill is held to the light.

Faint background colors are printed on the bill. Without the proper inks and printing machines, these are hard to copy.

Color-shifting ink is used to print the number 20 in the lower right corner. When the bill is moved, the color-shifting ink changes color.

Plastic cards

Coins and bills are a convenient and trustworthy means of carrying and using money, but many people rarely use cash today. Modern cashless forms of money make it easier for people to make and accept payments.

One of the most popular ways of banking and making payments today is with special plastic cards. Computers record the **transactions**. Plastic cards are issued by banks and other businesses.

Debit cards

People can use debit cards to pay for products and services with electronic funds transfer at point of sale, or EFTPOS. To make a payment, a person swipes their card through a small machine, chooses the type of account they have, then enters a personal identification number, or PIN. The money is moved from their account electronically. People can also withdraw cash when paying for products and services with EFTPOS.

People can use their debit cards and PINs to withdraw or deposit cash, or to deposit a check in **automatic teller machines**, or **ATMs**.

A man uses his plastic card to withdraw money from an ATM.

Credit cards

Some plastic cards are credit cards. Buying on credit means buying something now and promising that you will pay for it later. Many credit cards have a credit limit. When a person reaches the credit limit on their card, they cannot buy anything else with that card until they have paid off some of their credit-card debt.

People with credit cards are sent regular statements. A statement lists the products and services that a person has bought using their credit card. The statement also lists how much is owing on the card, and when a payment must be made.

Credit-card debt

Banks and other businesses that issue credit cards make money from the cards. They do this by charging **interest**. The larger your debt, the more interest you pay. Some people with large credit-card debts find it hard to pay the money back.

Credit cards should be used wisely, to avoid creating large debts that cannot be repaid.

The first banks

Banks are businesses that store money for customers and lend money to customers. Banks also offer other services, such as changing money from one currency into another.

Long ago, the first banks were set up in palaces, temples, and government warehouses. People deposited valuable products, such as grain and cattle, and received a receipt. A person could use the receipt to take back their products, or pass the receipt to another person as a form of payment.

Changes to banks

Over time, banks were set up in their own buildings. These buildings had to be secure, because they held valuables. People deposited precious metals, coins, and bills. They knew that the banks could keep their valuables safe.

Handwritten receipts became special books called passbooks. When a person made a deposit or withdrawal, a teller who worked in the bank would write the transaction in the passbook.

Passbooks were once used to record a person's account details and transactions.

Modern banking

Most people today have bank accounts, but many people rarely step inside a bank. That is because it is possible to do most banking electronically. Many people have their **salaries** paid directly into their bank accounts. Money can be transferred, and bills can be paid, over the telephone, or on the Internet. People can withdraw or deposit cash using ATMs.

Central banks

Most countries have a central bank that is owned by the government. A central bank makes and issues coins and bills, and holds the government's money. A central bank is not the same as a commercial bank, which is where most people have their bank accounts.

Info-plus!

Banks pay interest on deposits but charge fees for their services. Banks also make money by **investing** some of the deposits.

Today, people can use their credit cards to pay bills or buy products over the telephone.

Changes to coins and bills

The look and security features of coins and bills are changed from time to time. Sometimes new currencies are created.

Changes to United States money

The United States has begun redesigning its paper bills to improve the security features. Some new design features will also help people, such as the visually impaired, tell denominations apart.

In October 2003, the United States issued a new $20 bill. This was the first of its redesigned bills. In September 2004, a new $50 bill was issued. The pictures from the previous bills are used on the redesigned bills, but small changes to them have been made so that they are harder to copy.

Previous bills were black and green. The new bills have extra background colors.

Info-plus!

In 2006, a new $10 bill was issued, and there are plans to issue a new $100 bill. There are no plans to redesign the $1, $2, and $5 bills.

In 2004, the United States issued a $50 bill with a new design that includes new security features.

The previous $50 bill was issued in 1997, and was black and green.

Changes to Australian money

Australia's bills used to be made from paper. Today, they are made from polymer. Bills made from polymer contain security features that make them hard to counterfeit.

Other advantages of polymer bills are that they last longer than paper bills, and they stay cleaner. Old or damaged polymer bills can be recycled into other products, such as plant pots.

Info-plus!

In Australia, the $1 bill was replaced by the $1 coin in 1984, and the $2 bill was replaced by the $2 coin in 1988. The paper bills lasted only about eight months, but the coins should last for 30 years.

Before 1988, all Australian bills were made from paper.

Australia issued its first polymer bill, a $10 bill, in January 1988.

Changes to Canadian money

It is expensive to make coins, so mints are always looking for ways to save money. In Canada, the 10-cent, 25-cent, and 50-cent coins used to be made of **nickel.** The 5-cent coin was made of copper and nickel. In 2000, the Royal Canadian Mint started minting these coins with a steel core that was covered, or plated, in nickel. The new nickel-plated coins are cheaper to make and last longer.

The new nickel-plated coins are also lighter than the older coins. Vending machines in Canada had to be altered so they could take the lighter coins.

Info-plus!

In many countries, all bills are legal tender but coins are legal tender only in limited amounts. In Canada, 5-cent coins are legal tender only up to a total of $5. A person may legally refuse to accept payment made in 101 5-cent coins.

Canada's new 5-cent coins have a steel core that is plated in nickel.

Changes to European currencies

Sometimes, old currencies are replaced with new currencies. In January 2002, 12 countries in western Europe began using a single currency called the euro. These countries are Austria, Belgium, Finland, France, Germany, Greece, Italy, Ireland, Luxembourg, the Netherlands, Portugal, and Spain. They are members of an organization called the European Union, or EU. Before the introduction of the euro, each of these countries had its own currency.

People can now move between these 12 countries without needing to change their money into another currency. They can easily compare the prices of goods and services in the **euro area**. A single currency makes doing business in the euro area easier.

The euro symbol is €. There are eight denominations of euro coins, and seven denominations of euro bills.

The euro is used by more than 300 million Europeans.

Info-plus!

Other European countries are also members of the EU. These countries may join the euro area in the future.

27

Money in the future

Today, people can buy and sell most products and services without using coins and bills. Plastic cards, computers, telephones, and the Internet make it possible to use money without handling cash. A lot of money in the future will be electronic money that is stored in computers. Some of the computers will be in small portable cards or tags.

Fewer world currencies

In the future, there may be fewer currencies in the world. Many countries in western Europe already use a single currency, the euro. Perhaps one day there will be one world currency.

The future of cash

People are using less cash. They can already shop from work or home, by ordering products over the telephone or Internet and paying for them electronically. This means that less cash will probably need to be made in the future.

Transfer - enter details

1. **From account:** * Select >>

   Your transaction description: This description will appear on your receipt/ statement.

2. **To account or group:** * Select >>

   ● Account

   ○ New account   Details will be added to your account address book.

   Account name:
   BSB:
   Account number:

3. **Amount:** * $ Not required when transferring to a transfer group.

   To account description: This description will appear on the account statement where money is being transferred.

   ● Transfer now
   ○ Once on: (dd/mm/yyyy)
   ○ Frequency: Select >>

   Start: (dd/mm/yyyy)

4. **When:** *

   End: ○ No end date
   OR
   ○ End after: transfers
   OR
   ○ End on: (dd/mm/yyyy)

   Transfer   Clear

Many people already do their banking over the Internet.

Smart cards

In the future, there will be new types of plastic cards. The smart card is already used in some countries. It is a plastic card that contains a computer chip. The computer chip holds information.

There are different types of smart cards. Some smart cards only store information. Other smart cards have computer chips that can store, add, and remove information. These cards can hold a person's bank account details, and can be used to make and record purchases and payments.

Info-plus!

A telephone card is one type of smart card. When a person buys a telephone card, the purchase price buys a set amount of credit. The person can use the card in public telephones many times, until the credit is used up.

This smart card contains both a computer chip and a magnetic stripe, enabling it to be used by a large number of stores.

Make your own bill

You can make your own bill featuring your portrait.

You will need:

- two sheets of paper
- colored pencils
- ruler
- eraser
- scissors

What to do:

1 Design your bill on one sheet of paper. Do a rough sketch of your portrait, then add other images that reflect you and your interests. Decide on the colors and words.

2 Use a dark-colored pencil and a ruler to draw a rectangle in the middle of the other sheet of paper. This is the outline of your bill.

3 Sketch your portrait inside the outline.

4 Add the words and other images. Make sure to include the denomination of the note and the name of an imaginary country.

5 Color your bill.

6 Cut out your bill.

Glossary

automatic teller machines, or ATMs machines used by customers with a banking card, to withdraw money or do other banking

blanks blank pieces of metal used to make coins

coining press a machine in which blank pieces of metal are hit with dies to make coins

debts money owed

denominations values shown on coins and bills

dies metal tools used to stamp designs on coins

drawer a person who makes a payment by check, and has the amount that is written on the check taken out of their bank account

electrum a natural mixture of gold and silver

embossing a technique that creates raised patterns on materials such as paper and plastic

euro area the area in western Europe where the euro is the single currency

interest money paid to a bank account-holder for using their money, or money charged to a borrower

investing a way of earning money by putting money into businesses

issues gives out, distributes

mints buildings where coins are made

nickel a type of metal

precious metals valuable metals, such as gold and silver

products objects that are bought, sold, or bartered

receipts special notes that prove someone has received money or products, or that someone has bought something

salaries set amounts of money that are paid regularly to employees for their work

services work that people pay others to do or provide

traders people who buy, sell, or exchange products or services

transactions some items of business that are done, such as making deposits or purchases

value the worth of something

Index